Cat Facts

Interesting Cat Fun Facts And Trivia You Probably Don't Know Before

[Fun Fact Books - 2]

Megan Parker

Cat Facts

Interesting Cat Fun Facts And Trivia You Probably Don't Know Before

(Facts Books Series – No.2)

Cat Facts

1. Americans truly love their pet cats. There are approximately 14 million more domestic cats than dogs in the US.

2. Male cats are also called toms and females are called queens or mollies.

3. The maxim, 'A cat always lands on its feet' isn't just an old myth. Some cats have fallen from more than

320 meters height onto concrete and come away unharmed.

4. There's a reason why cats are likely to sustain high falls – they have enough time to prepare for the landing.

5. It's not a flock, it's not a herd – a group of cats together is also known as a 'clowder'.

6. According to analytics, cat owners are healthier than those without cats. The risk of heart attack is cut by a third among people who have cat as their pet.

7. Just like a dog's bark has several different meanings, a cat may purr because it is nervous, happy or feeling unwell.

8. It's common knowledge that cats like milk, but the fact is many of them are lactose intolerant. It means that they are actually allergic to milk.

9. Garfield, the cat lover with the lasagna, was featured in the Guinness Book of World Records because it was the most widespread cartoon.

10. Cats are considered pretty smart, and with a brain that is 90% similar to the human brain, it's no surprise.

11. When Abraham Lincoln was the American president, he had four cats who lived with him in the White House.

12. Felicette was the first feline to make a trip to space. Fortunately, she survived the mission and was nicknamed 'Astrocat'.

13. If you consider yourself a 'cat person', you belong to 11.5% of the people in the world.

14. If you are a man with a cat, you are more likely to find true love. This is due to the fact that people who see cat owners are friendly, reliable and sensitive.

15. The record for the largest number of kittens in the same litter was 19.

16. During her life, a cat named Dusty had a total of 420 kittens.

17. The oldest cat to give birth to kittens was called Kitty. She was 30 years old when she got her last kittens.

18. Bagpuss was a 1999 TV show that featured an old cloth cat. In 2001, it became the fourth in a poll of the largest children's TV shows.

19. While people dote about their cats in the West, about 4 million cats are killed and eaten in Asia.

20. There are around 70 different cat breeds and no less than 500 million pet cats in the world.

21. Ancient Egyptians worshiped a goddess who was half a cat and half a woman.

22. In Ancient Egypt, civilians would suffer a severe punishment if they hurt a cat.

23. Have you ever noticed that your cat sleeps most of the time? On average, cats sleep around 16 hours a day.

24. Kittens sleep even more often, since growth hormones are released when they are sleep.

25. The front paws of a cat are different from the back paws. They have 5 toes on the front but only 4 on the back.

26. Some cats are known as "polydactyl' and have extra toes. Some polydactyl have as many as 8 toes per paw.

27. Unlike dogs, cats have no sense of what is sweet. No wonder they never seem happy with cakes!

28. Did you think the cat flap was an ultramodern idea? Isaac Newton is credited with the invention of the cat flap - something that most cat owners now have.

29. Isaac Newton himself had a cat named Spithead, who influenced his invention. Spithead continued with kittens, who all got their own cat flap.

30. Many cat owners take their pets to the vet to be neutered, thereby increasing their pet's life expectancy by 2-3 years.

31. Cats can see very well in the dark, which explains why they always roam around at night.

32. Adolf Hitler hated cats, so there is another reason why you don't like him.

33. Taurine is an amino acid that can be found in cat food. Without this substance your cat would eventually become blind.

34. Domestic cats can run at a speed of 30 miles per hour.

35. The kidneys of a cat are pretty amazing because they can filter water before they are used. This means that a cat can drink sea water and the salt will be filtered out.

36. Those cute hairy pieces in a cat's ear are called "ear furnishings." They ensure that dirt does not enter and also helps them hear well.

37. Cats have good hearing and can hear ultrasonic sounds. They may hear dolphins.

38. It is not only people who are right-handed or left-handed. Most female cats prefer the use of their right leg, while men are more likely to be 'left pawed'.

39. A 'haw' is the third eyelid of a cat, which can only be seen if the cat is not good.

40. They may have an extra eyelid, but they don't have eyelashes.

41. The original version of Cinderella in Italy had a cat as the fairy godmother.

42. Dogs make 10 different sounds, while cats can make 100 different sounds.

43. Cats look like such lovely creatures, but around 40,000 people suffer from cat bites in America every year.

44. When you see a cat rubbing against a person, it is being affectionate, but also making its territory to make other cats aware.

45. The cat family consists of many different animals, but the largest is the Siberian tiger, which can be as tall as 12 feet.

46. The black-footed cat is the smallest wild cat, which is only 20 inches long.

47. The richest cat ever was Blackie, a multi-millionaire. It owned £ 15 million after its wealthy owner died.

48. London was the home of the very first cat show. It took place in 1871 and started a trend that has continued since then.

49. While cats like to catch and eat mice, it is not necessarily a good meal. They can catch tapeworms by eating these rodents.

50. The hearts of cats beat at a speed of 110-140 beats per minute - about twice as fast as the average person.

51. Ancient Egyptian cat owners would shave their eyebrows if they mourn their dead cats.

52. "Mau" is the Egyptian word for cat, and the oldest existing cat breed is known as the Egyptian Mau, translated to mean "the Egyptian cat."

53. While people are reluctant to buy cats of other sexes, they will actually be better off with each other than those of the same sex.

54. If you own a cat, you should give them 10-20 small meals every day, instead of fewer and larger meals.

55. Cats should avoid poinsettia during the Christmas period because they are poisonous.

56. Stray and wild cats that live outside have a lifespan of about 4 years. Those who live indoors can live for up to 16 years or more.

57. Cats are fish lovers, but too much tuna can cause them to become addicted to this meat.

58. They use their tongues to thoroughly clean themselves, but they also use them to remove the human odor.

59. When cats are born for the first time, they have blue eyes. The color changes over time.

60. Kittens also have much sharper teeth than adult cats. Their teeth become blunt when they are about 6 months old.

61. Cats with blue eyes for the duration of their lives are probably deaf.

62. They usually hate water, but the Turkish Van cats actually enjoy getting wet!

63. Unlike many other animals, cats cannot produce fat themselves. It is important to give your pet a balanced diet with good fats.

64. Just as a person's fingerprints are unique, every cat has a completely different nose.

65. Many people are allergic to cats, but cats can also be allergic to humans. About one in 200 domestic cats suffers from asthma due to smoke, dust and other particles in houses.

66. As long as you introduce your cat to your dog before they are both six months old, they must approve.

67. Although studies suggested that cats did not enjoy being petted by humans, further research has proven that they actually like it.

68. A cat's brain is so fast that even a supercomputer could not beat it in 2015.

69. Wild cats go more often and much further than domestic cats. Domestic cats are normally found in the area where they live.

70. 55% of domestic cats are thought to be obese due to overeating.

71. Alzheimer's disease can be found in cats, just as it can be found in humans.

72. Cats were first domesticated in China around 5,000 years ago. Farmers were the first to realize that cats could be kept in the house.

73. In 2011, scientists concluded that your cat can become very ill if you disrupt its routine.

74. The high cry that you may have heard from your cat is an attempt for cats to go their own way. The cry is similar to that of a newborn baby.

75. Cats love to sit on warm objects, which is probably why your cat likes to sit on your computer.

76. It's a well-known fact that cats are very picky creatures, and if your pet doesn't always drink water

from the water bowl, it might not be as fun as the shape of the bowl!

77. Cats may seem harmless, but they have worked together to make more than 30 different species extinct. Even domestic cats love hunting, and have contributed heavily to this figure.

78. They only sweat through their legs, because this is the only place with sweat glands.

79. In the 1950s, Disneyland bought several cats to hunt mice at night. There are now more than 200 felines in the amusement park.

80. Their whiskers are used to measure holes and openings. They let the cat find out if they fit through spaces.

81. Historians believe that every species of the cat family came from one of only five different wild cats from Africa.

82. Female cats can breed with multiple males if they are heaters. This means that a litter of kittens could have a few different fathers!

83. A cat can turn each of its ears individually. Each ear has a total of 32 muscles.

84. Don't give chocolate to your cat, it's toxic.

85. Cats are pretty great when jumping; they can jump up to seven times higher than the length of their tail.

86. There is a charming reason why your cat brings dead mice to you. It means that your pet likes you!

87. They can't survive eating a vegetarian diet, so it's important to feed your cat meat.

88. Cats can find their way home even though they have traveled for miles.

89. Black cats are the least frequently adopted from an animal enclosure, although people love to buy black kittens.

90. The tail of a cat will tremble when he is near someone he loves.

91. Do you think your cat purrs a lot? Cats track up to 26 times per second.

92. Felines enjoy spending time alone. Unlike dogs, they don't need much attention and can be very happy without any company.

93. You don't have to feed many cats from the same food bowl. It is very likely that some of them will refuse to eat from it, but prefer to eat alone.

94. Don't look at your cat for a long time. This is seen as threatening and makes it uncomfortable.

95. There are many plants that are toxic to cats, although parsley, sage and other herbs are among the favorite foods of a cat.

96. If you put a collar on your cat, make sure it is not too tight. You should be able to fit two fingers between

the collar and the neck of your cat, otherwise you could take the risk of strangling it.

97. The fear of cats is known as Ailurophobia.

98. A town called Talkeetna in Alaska had a cat as mayor for 15 years.

99. The record for the world's tallest cat was 48.5 centimeters.

100. Cats recognize the voices of their owners, but often behave as if they don't care.

Finally, if you like this book, then I'd like to ask you for a favor, would you be kind enough to leave a review for this book on Amazon? It will be great help to reach more number of readers like you!

Please leave a review for this book on Amazon!

Thank you and good luck!

Bestsellers Books about Facts and Trivia

1) 700+ Random Harry Potter Fun Facts and Trivia: Interesting Harry Potter Fun Facts and Trivia You Probably Don't Know

Check Out Here -

https://www.amazon.com/dp/1729036864

2) Random Animal Facts You Probably Don't Know (Facts Books Series)

Check Out Here -

https://www.amazon.com/dp/1790694078

Printed in Great Britain
by Amazon

23979604R00020